CENTRAL
EUROPE

EASTERN EUROPE

EAST AND
SOUTHEAST ASIA

MIDDLE EAST

NORTH
EAST AFRICA

WESTERN AND
SOUTHERN ASIA

CENTRAL
AND
SOUTHERN
AFRICA

OCEANIA

Compiled by Gaby Goldsack
Illustrated by Martin Cater
Consultant: Michael Faul, The Flag Institute, UK

This is a Parragon Publishing book
This edition published in 2004

Parragon Publishing
Queen Street House
4 Queen Street
Bath BA1 1HE, UK

Copyright © Parragon 2004

ISBN 1-40543-066-4

Printed in Indonesia

FLAGS
OF THE
WORLD

CONTENTS

ABOUT FLAGS

VEXILLUM

TRIANGULAR PENNON

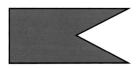

SWALLOW-TAILED PENNON

THE JOLLY ROGER

THE RED FLAG (COMMUNIST)

AFRICAN NATIONAL CONGRESS

The earliest known cloth flags are believed to have come from China. They were often sewn from different pieces of cloth and embroidered or painted with royal emblems. In Western Europe during the Roman Empire the vexillum was carried by the Roman Cavalry standard bearer.

In the Middle Ages, the Crusaders carried a lance into battle with a pennon attached. These were triangular or swallow-tailed in shape.

During the 1600s, some pirate captains of the Caribbean flew their own flags, including the infamous "Jolly Roger," as a signal that they would board and plunder ships.

Ships have always relied on flags for identification at sea and for sending messages to other ships, especially during battle. Over the centuries a signal flag code developed, which is now internationally recognized.

Flags often tell a story about the past, present, and future hopes of a population. During the 1700-1900s, many countries fought to establish nation states, and the flag became a source of national pride. Some flags, such as the communist flag and the ANC flag, have come to represent wider political struggles.

Most of the flags in this book are national flags. There are 192 officially recognized countries in the world, but there are many more flags. Provinces, states, territories, cities, and organizations can all have flags as part of their identity. Some disputed territories have flags.

Each flag in this book shows the following information:

1. NAME OF COUNTRY The number appears on the map to show where the country is

Ratio: The relationship between the flag's height and width giving its shape .
Date adopted: The date the flag was officially recognized.
Capital: The city from which the country is governed. This is shown on the map as a red dot ●
Population: The number of people living in the country when this book was published.
Currency: The money used within the country.

A brief description of what each flag stands for.

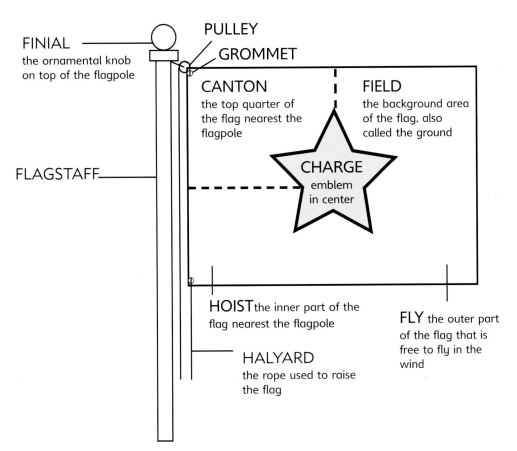

FINIAL
the ornamental knob
on top of the flagpole

PULLEY

GROMMET

CANTON
the top quarter of
the flag nearest the
flagpole

FIELD
the background area
of the flag, also
called the ground

CHARGE
emblem
in center

FLAGSTAFF

HOIST the inner part of the
flag nearest the flagpole

FLY the outer part
of the flag that is
free to fly in the
wind

HALYARD
the rope used to raise
the flag

TYPES OF FLAGS

These days, most flags are square or rectangular, but there are a variety of rectangular shapes. The shape of a flag is described as a ratio. This is the relationship between the flag's height and width. For example, if the flag's ratio is 1:2, it will be twice as wide as it is high.

Many flags display different colors in stripes or blocks with an emblem at the center. Here are some of the more common patterns:

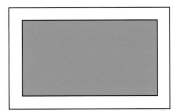

BORDER a strip of color that runs around the outer edge of the flag

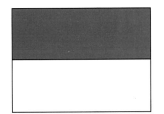

BICOLOR two bands of color either horizontal or vertical

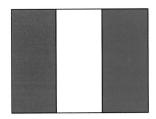

TRICOLOR three bands of different colors either horizontal or vertical

QUARTERED a field divided into four equal quarters

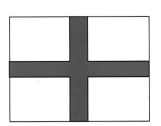

CROSS a centred cross that divides the field

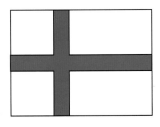

SCANDINAVIAN CROSS a cross that divides the field where the vertical is to the left of center

SALTIRE an X-shaped cross

COUPED CROSS a complete cross surrounded by the field where the arms are equal

TRIANGLE a triangle of any shape or size

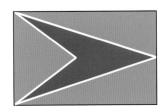

FIMBRIATION a narrow band that acts as a border between two colors

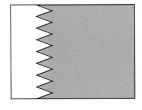

SERRATION a zigzag edge like the teeth on a saw

NORTH AND CENTRAL AMERICA

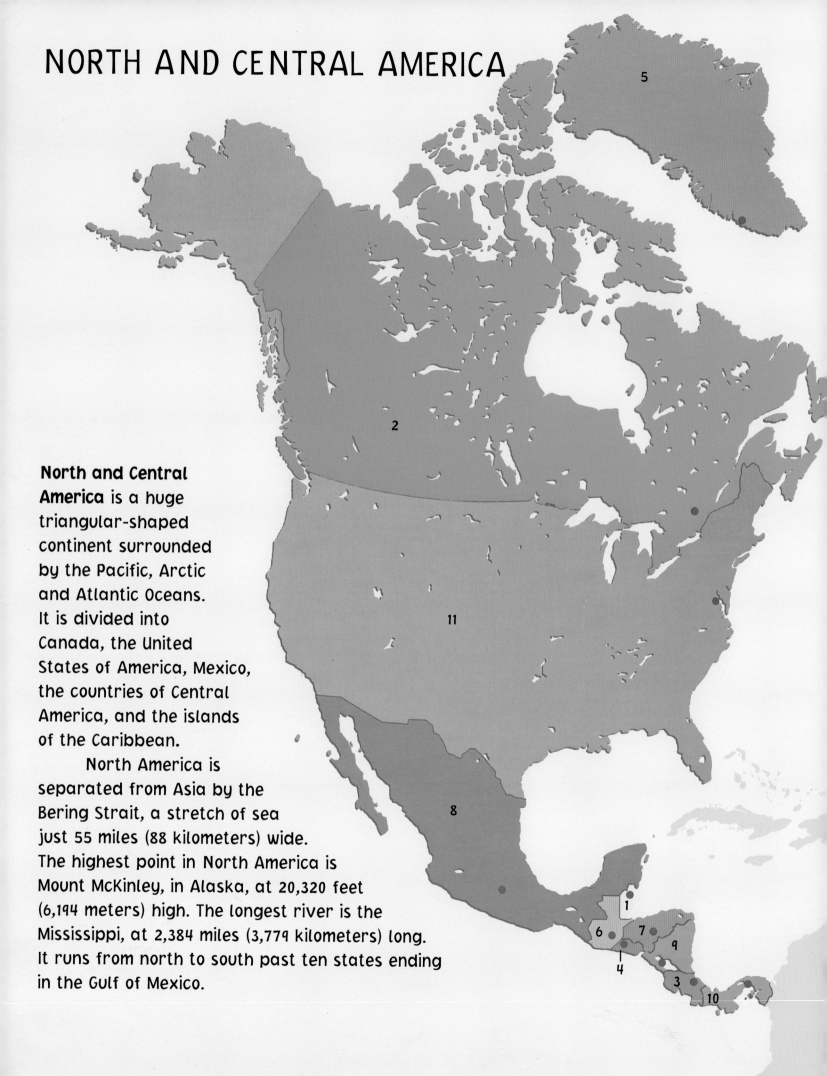

North and Central America is a huge triangular-shaped continent surrounded by the Pacific, Arctic and Atlantic Oceans. It is divided into Canada, the United States of America, Mexico, the countries of Central America, and the islands of the Caribbean.

North America is separated from Asia by the Bering Strait, a stretch of sea just 55 miles (88 kilometers) wide. The highest point in North America is Mount McKinley, in Alaska, at 20,320 feet (6,194 meters) high. The longest river is the Mississippi, at 2,384 miles (3,779 kilometers) long. It runs from north to south past ten states ending in the Gulf of Mexico.

1. BELIZE

Ratio: 2:3
Date adopted: 1981
Capital: Belmopan
Population: 266,440
Currency: Belizean dollar

The coat of arms shows pictures from the country's timber trade.

2. CANADA

Ratio: 1:2
Date adopted: 1965
Capital: Ottawa
Population: 32,207,113
Currency: Canadian dollar

The eleven-pointed Maple Leaf has been Canada's national emblem since 1860.

3. COSTA RICA

Ratio: 3:5
Date adopted: 1848
Capital: San José
Population: 3,896,092
Currency: Costa Rican colón

Red was added to the Central American Federation flag to reflect the French tricolore.

4. EL SALVADOR

Ratio: 4:7
Date adopted: 1912
Capital: San Salvador
Population: 6,470,379
Currency: U.S. dollar

Many Central American flags use the colors of the former Central American Federation.

5. GREENLAND

Ratio: 2:3
Date adopted: 1985
Capital: Nuuk (Godthab)
Population: 56,385
Currency: Danish krone

Greenland is a self-governing territory of Denmark.

6. GUATEMALA

Ratio: 5:8
Date adopted: 1871
Capital: Guatemala City
Population: 13,909,384
Currency: Quetzal, U.S. dollar

The coat of arms features the quetzal, Guatemala's most famous bird.

7. HONDURAS

Ratio: 1:2
Date adopted: 1866
Capital: Tegucigalpa
Population: 6,669,789
Currency: Lempira

The stars represent the five original members of the former Central American Federation.

8. MEXICO

Ratio: 4:7
Date adopted: 1968
Capital: Mexico City
Population: 104,907,991
Currency: Mexican peso

The eagle and cactus recall an Aztec legend about the founding of Mexico City.

9. NICARAGUA

Ratio: 3:5
Date adopted: 1908
Capital: Managua
Population: 5,128,517
Currency: Córdoba

Nicaragua retained the flag of the Central American Federation after it dissolved.

10. PANAMA

Ratio: 2:3
Date adopted: 1903
Capital: Panama City
Population: 2,960,784
Currency: Balboa, U.S. dollar

The colors represent two main political parties: blue for Conservative, red for Liberal.

11. UNITED STATES OF AMERICA

Ratio: 10:19
Date adopted: 1777
Capital: Washington, D.C.
Population: 290,342,554
Currency: U.S. dollar

The "Stars and Stripes" has 13 stripes for the original British colonies and 50 stars, one for each state.

THE CARIBBEAN

The islands of **The Caribbean** lie in the Caribbean Sea off the east coast of America. They include the group of islands known as the West Indies.

   Cuba, at 42,803 square miles (110,861 square kilometers), is as big as all the other islands combined, and is home to a third of the Caribbean population.

   From the 1400s onwards, European nations fought for control of this region, and it is only fairly recently that some countries have gained independence and flown their own flags.

1. ANTIGUA & BARBUDA

Ratio: 2:3
Date adopted: 1967
Capital: St. John's
Population: 67,897
Currency: East Caribbean dollar

This was the winning entry in a competition held in 1967.

2. THE BAHAMAS

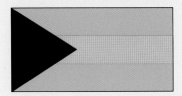

Ratio: 1:2
Date adopted: 1973
Capital: Nassau
Population: 297,477
Currency: Bahamian dollar

Yellow reflects the country's sand, blue its sea, black the pride of its people.

3. BARBADOS

Ratio: 2:3
Date adopted: 1966
Capital: Bridgetown
Population: 277,264
Currency: Barbadian dollar

Barbados' colonial flag, which featured Britannia holding a trident, inspired the central symbol.

4. CUBA

Ratio: 1:2
Date adopted: 1902
Capital: Havana
Population: 11,263,429
Currency: Cuban peso

Cuba adopted this flag in 1902 when it won independence from Spain.

5. DOMINICA

Ratio: 1:2
Date adopted: 1978
Capital: Roseau
Population: 69,655
Currency: East Caribbean dollar

The emblem features a sisserou parrot, the national bird, which is unique to Dominica.

6. DOMINICAN REPUBLIC

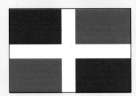

Ratio: 2:3
Date adopted: 1844
Capital: Santo Domingo
Population: 8,715,602
Currency: Dominican peso

This was designed by putting a white cross, representing Christian faith, on top of Haiti's flag.

7. GRENADA

Ratio: 3:5
Date adopted: 1974
Capital: St George's
Population: 89,258
Currency: East Caribbean dollar

The central star represents Grenada's capital. The stars represent its parishes. A nutmeg is also shown.

8. HAITI

Ratio: 3:5
Date adopted: 1820
Capital: Port-au-Prince
Population: 7,527,817
Currency: Gourde

This was sewn together from scraps of the French flag during the fight for independence from France.

9. JAMAICA

Ratio: 1:2
Date adopted: 1962
Capital: Kingston
Population: 2,695,867
Currency: Jamaican dollar

"Hardships there are but the land is green and the sun shineth", is how the locals explain this flag.

10. ST. KITTS & NEVIS

Ratio: 2:3
Date adopted: 1983
Capital: Basseterre
Population: 38,763
Currency: East Caribbean dollar

Its colors stand for fertile land, the sun, the struggle for freedom and the people's African heritage.

11. ST. LUCIA

Ratio: 1:2
Date adopted: 1979
Capital: Castries
Population: 162,157
Currency: East Caribbean dollar

Blue represents the sea, gold the sunshine, and black and white St. Lucia's people.

12. ST. VINCENT & THE GRENADINES

Ratio: 2:3
Date adopted: 1985
Capital: Kingstown
Population: 116,812
Currency: East Caribbean dollar

The three green diamonds in the centre of the flag form a letter "V" for Vincent.

13. TRINIDAD & TOBAGO

Ratio: 3:5
Date adopted: 1962
Capital: Port-of-Spain
Population: 1,104,209
Currency: Dollar

The black stripe stands for the people and for the republic's plentiful oil and gas.

SOUTH AMERICA

South America is linked to North America by the isthmus (a thin strip of land) of Panama. It is surrounded by the Atlantic Ocean, the Pacific Ocean and the Caribbean Sea.

The Andes, the world's longest mountain range, runs the length of the western coast. They rise to their highest point, 22,835 feet (6,970 meters), at Mount Aconcagua in Argentina.

The Amazon, the second longest river in the world at 4,080 miles (6,579 kilometers), runs from the Peruvian Andes to the Atlantic in Brazil. Brazil, which covers almost half the continent, is the largest country in South America.

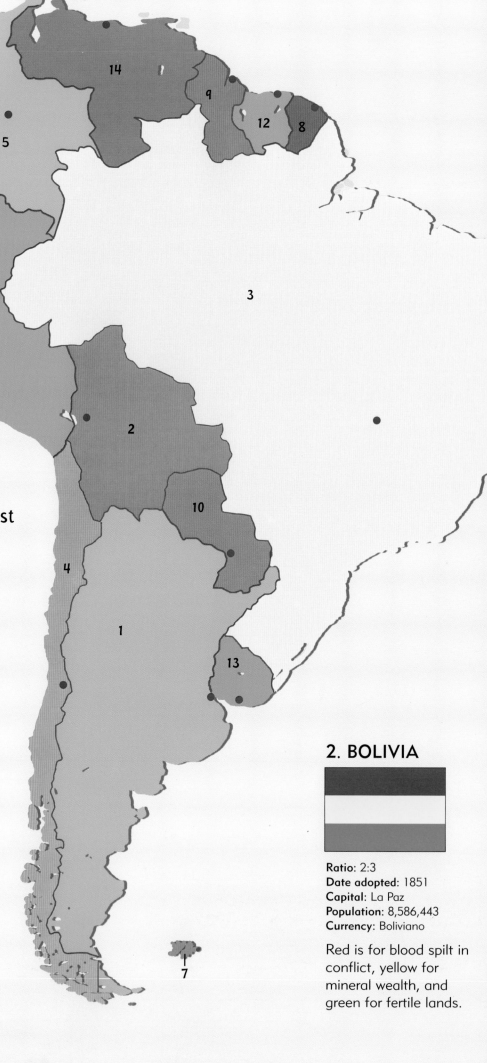

1. ARGENTINA

Ratio: 1:2
Date adopted: 1816
Capital: Buenos Aires
Population: 38,740,807
Currency: Argentine peso

The sun represents the sun that shone in May 1810 when rebels overthrew the Spanish.

2. BOLIVIA

Ratio: 2:3
Date adopted: 1851
Capital: La Paz
Population: 8,586,443
Currency: Boliviano

Red is for blood spilt in conflict, yellow for mineral wealth, and green for fertile lands.

3. BRAZIL

Ratio: 7:10
Date adopted: 1889
Capital: Brasilia
Population: 182,032,604
Currency: Real

Green and yellow are national colors. The stars represent the 27 states in the federation.

4. CHILE

Ratio: 2:3
Date adopted: 1823
Capital: Santiago
Population: 15,665,216
Currency: Chilean peso

This red, white, and blue flag dates back to the war of independence against Spain.

5. COLOMBIA

Ratio: 2:3
Date adopted: 1819
Capital: Bogotá
Population: 41,662,073
Currency: Colombian peso

This is very similar to the flags of Colombia's neighbors, Ecuador and Venezuela.

6. ECUADOR

Ratio: 1:2
Date adopted: 1860
Capital: Quito
Population: 13,710,234
Currency: U.S. dollar

The coat of arms, topped by a condor, distinguishes this from the Colombian flag.

7. FALKLAND ISLANDS

Ratio: 1:2
Date adopted: 1948
Capital: Stanley
Population: 2,967
Currency: Falkland pound

The islands' status as a British territory is disputed by Argentina, where they are called Islas Malvinas.

8. FRENCH GUIANA

Ratio: 2:3
Date adopted: –
Capital: Cayenne
Population: 186,917
Currency: Euro, French franc

As a territory of France, the official flag is the French tricolore.

9. GUYANA

Ratio: 3:5
Date adopted: 1966
Capital: Georgetown
Population: 702,100
Currency: Guyanese dollar

It is easy to see why Guyana's flag is nicknamed "the Golden Arrow."

10. PARAGUAY

Ratio: 1:2
Date adopted: 1842
Capital: Asunción
Population: 6,036,900
Currency: Guarani

This flag, based on the French tricolore, has different emblems on each side.

11. PERU

Ratio: 2:3
Date adopted: 1825
Capital: Lima
Population: 24,409,897
Currency: Sol

The red and white are said to have been inspired by a flock of flying flamingos.

12. SURINAME

Ratio: 2:3
Date adopted: 1975
Capital: Paramaribo
Population: 435,449
Currency: Suriname guilder

The yellow star represents unity between Suriname's five peoples.

13. URUGUAY

Ratio: 2:3
Date adopted: 1830
Capital: Montevideo
Population: 3,413,329
Currency: Uruguayan peso

This is based on the flag of Argentina, the first independent South American nation.

14. VENEZUELA

Ratio: 2:3
Date adopted: 1930
Capital: Caracas
Population: 24,654,694
Currency: Bolivar

The arc of seven stars represents the seven provinces that supported independence.

WESTERN EUROPE

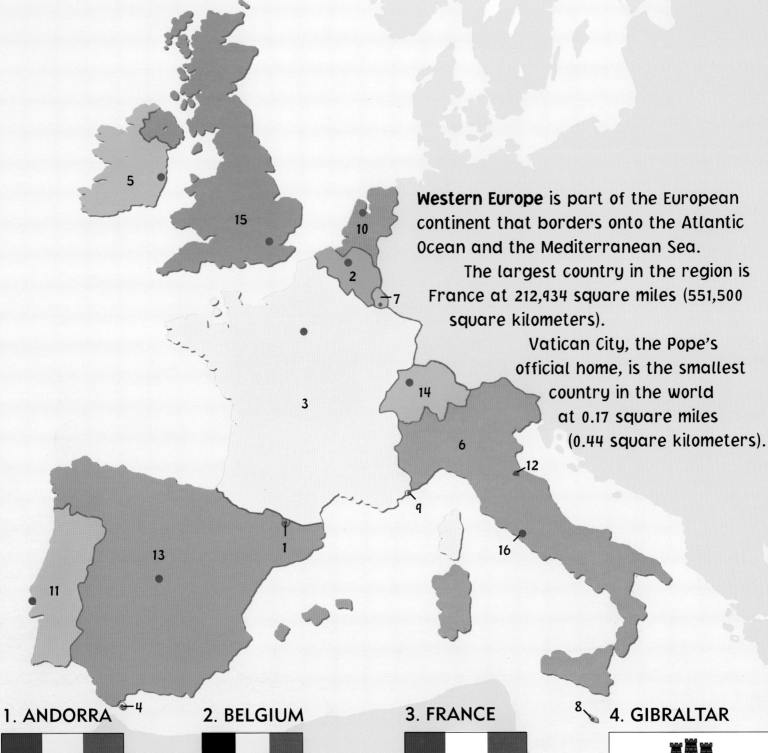

Western Europe is part of the European continent that borders onto the Atlantic Ocean and the Mediterranean Sea.

The largest country in the region is France at 212,934 square miles (551,500 square kilometers).

Vatican City, the Pope's official home, is the smallest country in the world at 0.17 square miles (0.44 square kilometers).

1. ANDORRA

Ratio: 2:3
Date adopted: 1866
Capital: Andorra la Vella
Population: 69,150
Currency: Euro

These colors reflect Adorra's link with its neighboring countries, France and Spain.

2. BELGIUM

Ratio: 13:15
Date adopted: 1831
Capital: Brussels
Population: 10,289,088
Currency: Euro

The colors come from a 13th-century coat of arms which featured a gold and red lion on black.

3. FRANCE

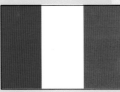

Ratio: 2:3
Date adopted: 1794
Capital: Paris
Population: 60,180,529
Currency: Euro

This flag was first used in the French Revolution, to represent liberty, equality, and fraternity.

4. GIBRALTAR

Ratio: 1:2
Date adopted: 1982
Capital: Gibraltar Town
Population: 27,776
Currency: Gibraltar pound

Although it is a British territory, the coat of arms shows its historical link with Spain.

5. REPUBLIC OF IRELAND

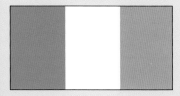

Ratio: 1:2
Date adopted: 1920
Capital: Dublin
Population: 3,924,140
Currency: Euro

The green stands for Roman Catholics, the orange for Protestants, and the white for peace.

6. ITALY

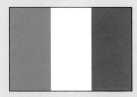

Ratio: 2:3
Date adopted: 1946
Capital: Rome
Population: 57,998,353
Currency: Euro

This flag is based on the standard designed by Napoleon during the Italian campaign of 1796.

7. LUXEMBOURG

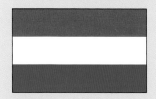

Ratio: 3:5
Date adopted: 1972
Capital: Luxembourg
Population: 454,157
Currency: Euro

This horizontal tricolor was first used in 1848, but it was not officially adopted until 1972.

8. MALTA

Ratio: 2:3
Date adopted: 1964
Capital: Valletta
Population: 400,420
Currency: Maltese lira

The George Cross was added after it was awarded to the islanders by George VI of Britain.

9. MONACO

Ratio: 4:5
Date adopted: 1881
Capital: Monaco-Ville
Population: 32,130
Currency: Euro

Red and white comes from the coat of arms of the Grimaldi family, the long-time rulers.

10. NETHERLANDS

Ratio: 2:3
Date adopted: 1937
Capital: Amsterdam
Population: 16,150,511
Currency: Euro

This flag was based on the livery of William of Orange, the first ruler of the Dutch Republic.

11. PORTUGAL

Ratio: 2:3
Date adopted: 1911
Capital: Lisbon
Population: 10,102,022
Currency: Euro

The navigational device behind the coat of arms is to symbolize its role in global exploration.

12. SAN MARINO

Ratio: 3:4
Date adopted: 1862
Capital: San Marino
Population: 28,119
Currency: Euro

The colours represent the peaks of Monte Titano, San Marino's highest mountain.

13. SPAIN

Ratio: 2:3
Date adopted: 1981
Capital: Madrid
Population: 40,217,413
Currency: Euro

Red and yellow was first used in 1785 to distinguish Spanish ships from others.

14. SWITZERLAND

Ratio: 1:1
Date adopted: 1889
Capital: Berne
Population: 7,318,638
Currency: Swiss franc

A white cross on a red background has been used on the Swiss flag since 1339.

15. UNITED KINGDOM

Ratio: 1:2
Date adopted: 1801
Capital: London
Population: 60,094,648
Currency: Pound sterling

The "Union Jack" is made up of three crosses, representing England, Scotland, and Ireland.

16. VATICAN CITY

Ratio: 1:1
Date adopted: 1929
Capital: The Vatican
Population: 911
Currency: Euro

This flag belonging to the Pope's official home includes the crossed papal keys.

CENTRAL EUROPE

Central Europe underwent many changes at the end of the last century.

In 1991 Estonia, Latvia, and Lithuania became independent of the Soviet Union.

In 1993 Czechoslovakia split into two states, the Czech Republic and Slovakia. These political upheavals have changed the national flags.

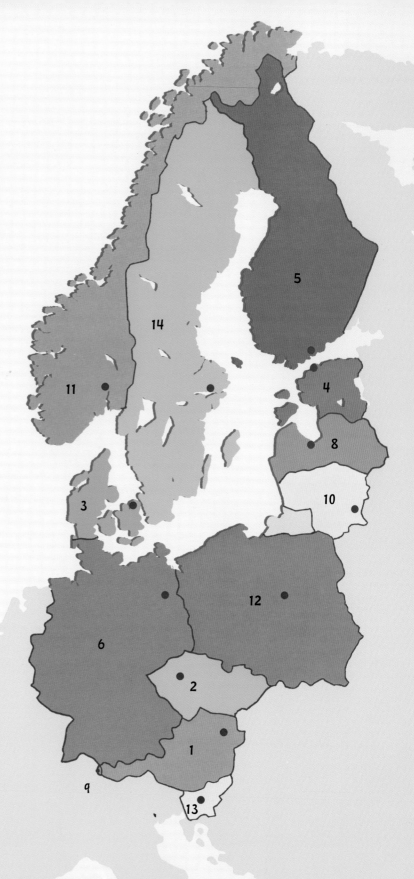

1. AUSTRIA

Ratio: 2:3
Date adopted: 1919
Capital: Vienna
Population: 8,188,207
Currency: Euro

This is supposedly styled on a duke's blood-stained tunic.

2. CZECH REPUBLIC

Ratio: 2:3
Date adopted: 1920
Capital: Prague
Population: 10,249,216
Currency: Koruna

When the Czech Republic split from Slovakia, it kept the flag.

3. DENMARK

Ratio: 28:37
Date adopted: 1625
Capital: Copenhagen
Population: 5,384,384
Currency: Danish krone

This flag, with its white cross, is thought to be Europe's oldest.

4. ESTONIA

Ratio: 7:11
Date adopted: 1918
Capital: Tallinn
Population: 1,408,556
Currency: Kroon

This was banned under Soviet rule but readopted in 1990.

5. FINLAND

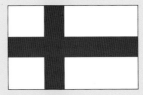

Ratio: 11:18
Date adopted: 1920
Capital: Helsinki
Population: 5,190,785
Currency: Euro

The blue is for Finland's many lakes. The white represents its snow.

6. GERMANY

Ratio: 3:5
Date adopted: 1919
Capital: Berlin
Population: 82,398,326
Currency: Euro

This historic flag now represents a united Germany.

7. ICELAND

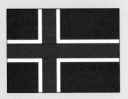

Ratio: 18:25
Date adopted: 1915
Capital: Reykjavik
Population: 280,798
Currency: Krona

Blue symbolizes its ocean, white its snow, and red its volcanoes.

8. LATVIA

Ratio: 1:2
Date adopted: 1918
Capital: Riga
Population: 2,348,784
Currency: Lat

Banned under Soviet rule, this flag was reintroduced in 1990.

9. LIECHTENSTEIN

Ratio: 3:5
Date adopted: 1937
Capital: Vaduz
Population: 33,145
Currency: Swiss franc

The crown was added in 1937 to differentiate it from the flag of Haiti.

10. LITHUANIA

Ratio: 1:2
Date adopted: 1918
Capital: Vilnius
Population: 3,592,561
Currency: Litas

Lithuania reverted to these traditional colours just before independence.

11. NORWAY

Ratio: 8:11
Date adopted: 1821
Capital: Oslo
Population: 4,546,123
Currency: Norwegian krone

Designed in 1821, this flag was officially adopted in 1898.

12. POLAND

Ratio: 5:8
Date adopted: 1919
Capital: Warsaw
Population: 38,622,660
Currency: Zloty

Red and white has been used on the Polish flag since the 1600s.

13. SLOVENIA

Ratio: 1:2
Date adopted: 1991
Capital: Ljubljana
Population: 1,935,677
Currency: Slovene tolar

The coat of arms featuring the three peaks of Mount Triglav was added upon independence.

14. SWEDEN

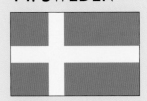

Ratio: 5:8
Date adopted: 1906
Capital: Stockholm
Population: 8,878,085
Currency: Swedish krona

This Scandinavian cross is borrowed from the Danish flag.

EASTERN EUROPE

Eastern Europe has seen many changes since the end of communism in the Soviet Union in the early 1990s.

Many countries, such as Macedonia and Slovakia, have become independent. New flags have been created or reinstated as symbols of new nations' sovereignty.

The Russian Federation, which stretches for 6,592,800 square miles (17,075,400 square kilometers), is the largest country in the world.

1. ALBANIA

Ratio: 5:7
Date adopted: 1992
Capital: Tirana
Population: 3,582,205
Currency: Lek

The black eagle has been used on Albanian flags since the 15th century.

2. ARMENIA

Ratio: 1:2
Date adopted: 1918
Capital: Yerevan
Population: 3,326,448
Currency: Dram

Red stands for blood spilled during conflict, blue for the sky, orange for fertile lands.

3. BELARUS

Ratio: 1:2
Date adopted: 1995
Capital: Minsk
Population: 10,322,151
Currency: Ruble

The decorative border is based on a traditional folk pattern of the region.

4. BOSNIA & HERZEGOVINA

Ratio: 1:2
Date adopted: 1998
Capital: Sarajevo
Population: 3,989,018
Currency: Marka

The blue background and stars come from the flag of the European Union.

5. BULGARIA

Ratio: 3:5
Date adopted: 1879
Capital: Sofia
Population: 7,537,929
Currency: Lev

This flag was reintroduced in 1990 after the collapse of communism.

6. CROATIA

Ratio: 1:2
Date adopted: 1990
Capital: Zagreb
Population: 4,422,248
Currency: Kuna

The red and white checks on the shield are Croatia's traditional emblem.

7. GEORGIA

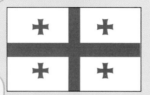

Ratio: 3:5
Date adopted: 1918
Capital: Tbilisi
Population: 4,934,413
Currency: Lari

Georgia has adopted the "Flag of Queen Tamar", a 13th century queen of Georgia.

8. GREECE

Ratio: 2:3
Date adopted: 1922
Capital: Athens
Population: 10,665,989
Currency: Euro

The white cross represents the Greek Orthodox Church, the main church in Greece.

9. HUNGARY

Ratio: 2:3
Date adopted: 1848
Capital: Budapest
Population: 10,045,407
Currency: Forint

Red symbolizes strength, white represents faithfulness, and green stands for hope.

10. MACEDONIA

Ratio: 1:2
Date adopted: 1995
Capital: Skopje
Population: 2,063,122
Currency: Macedonian denar

This eight-rayed, golden-yellow sun replaced the "Star of Vergina" in 1995.

11. MOLDOVA

Ratio: 1:2
Date adopted: 1990
Capital: Chisinau
Population: 4,439,502
Currency: Moldovan leu

The colors are the same as Romania's, but Moldova has added its coat of arms.

12. ROMANIA

Ratio: 2:3
Date adopted: 1861
Capital: Bucharest
Population: 22,271,839
Currency: Romanian leu

This flag was reintroduced after the collapse of the communist regime in 1989.

13. RUSSIAN FEDERATION

Ratio: 2:3
Date adopted: 1991
Capital: Moscow
Population: 144,526,278
Currency: Ruble

Russia's colors have influenced many Eastern European flags.

14. SERBIA & MONTENEGRO

Ratio: 1:2
Date adopted: 1992
Capital: Belgrade
Population: 10,655,774
Currency: Dinar

To distinguish it from others, the order of the Slavic colors has been changed.

15. SLOVAKIA

Ratio: 2:3
Date adopted: 1993
Capital: Bratislava
Population: 5,430,033
Currency: Slovak koruna

This flag was adopted after the break up of Czechoslovakia.

16. UKRAINE

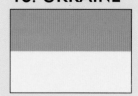

Ratio: 2:3
Date adopted: 1918
Capital: Kiev
Population: 48,055,439
Currency: Hryvnya

This traditional flag was reintroduced when the country gained independence in 1991.

THE MIDDLE EAST

The Middle East bridges the gap between Africa and Asia. Much of its landscape is either mountainous or hot, sandy desert. The Arabian Desert, spreads over 1 million square miles (1.6 million square kilometers), is the second largest desert in the world. It lies between the Red Sea and The Gulf.

1. AZERBAIJAN

Ratio: 1:2
Date adopted: 1991
Capital: Baku
Population: 7,830,764
Currency: Manat

The white crescent and star in the centre are traditional symbols of Islam.

2. BAHRAIN

Ratio: 3:5
Date adopted: 2002
Capital: Manama
Population: 667,238
Currency: Bahraini dinar

Red and white are traditional colours of the Gulf States around the Persian Gulf.

3. CYPRUS

Ratio: 3:5
Date adopted: 1960
Capital: Nicosia
Population: 771,657
Currency: Cyprus pound

At the centre of the flag is a copper silhouette of the island and an olive branch.

4. IRAN

Ratio: 4:7
Date adopted: 1980
Capital: Tehran
Population: 68,278,826
Currency: Rial

The colours represent the Islamic religion. The script repeats 'God is great' 22 times.

5. IRAO

Ratio: 2:3
Date adopted: 1991
Capital: Baghdad
Population: 24,683,313
Currency: Iraqi dinar

A recent attempt to change this flag was rejected by the Iraqi people.

6. ISRAEL

Ratio: 8:11
Date adopted: 1948
Capital: Jerusalem
Population: 6,116,533
Currency: New shekel

The 'Star of David', and blue and white colours are traditional symbols of the Jewish people.

7. JORDAN

Ratio: 1:2
Date adopted: 1928
Capital: Amman
Population: 5,460,265
Currency: Jordanian dinar

The star symbolizes the first seven verses of the Koran, the Islamic Holy Scriptures.

8. KUWAIT

Ratio: 1:2
Date adopted: 1961
Capital: Kuwait City
Population: 2,183,161
Currency: Kuwaiti dinar

This flag, with stripes and a trapezoid shape, is in traditional Pan-Arab colours.

9. LEBANON

Ratio: 2:3
Date adopted: 1943
Capital: Beirut
Population: 3,727,703
Currency: Lebanese pound

The central tree is the Cedar of Lebanon, the country's symbol since Biblical times.

10. OMAN

Ratio: 1:2
Date adopted: 1995
Capital: Muscat
Population: 2,807,125
Currency: Rial Omani

The coat of arms in the corner is made up of two crossed swords, a dagger and a belt.

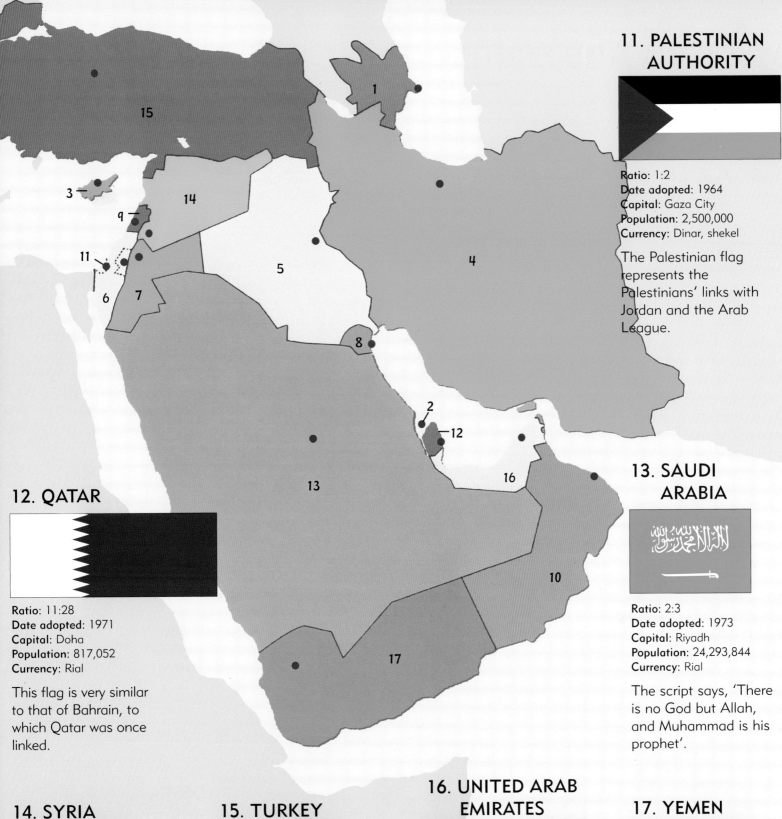

11. PALESTINIAN AUTHORITY

Ratio: 1:2
Date adopted: 1964
Capital: Gaza City
Population: 2,500,000
Currency: Dinar, shekel

The Palestinian flag represents the Palestinians' links with Jordan and the Arab League.

13. SAUDI ARABIA

Ratio: 2:3
Date adopted: 1973
Capital: Riyadh
Population: 24,293,844
Currency: Rial

The script says, 'There is no God but Allah, and Muhammad is his prophet'.

12. QATAR

Ratio: 11:28
Date adopted: 1971
Capital: Doha
Population: 817,052
Currency: Rial

This flag is very similar to that of Bahrain, to which Qatar was once linked.

14. SYRIA

Ratio: 2:3
Date adopted: 1958
Capital: Damascus
Population: 17,585,540
Currency: Syrian pound

The two green stars originally represented a union between Syria and Egypt.

15. TURKEY

Ratio: 2:3
Date adopted: 1936
Capital: Ankara
Population: 68,109,469
Currency: Turkish lira

The star and crescent moon are traditional symbols of the Islamic religion.

16. UNITED ARAB EMIRATES

Ratio: 1:2
Date adopted: 1971
Capital: Abu Dhabi
Population: 2,484,818
Currency: UAE dirham

These are the colours of Arab unity and nationalism.

17. YEMEN

Ratio: 2:3
Date adopted: 1990
Capital: Sanaa
Population: 19,349,881
Currency: Saudi rial

This tricolour flag was adopted when South Yemen united with North Yemen in 1990.

WESTERN AND SOUTHERN ASIA

Western and Southern Asia are part of the world's largest continent. This region of Asia is in the Indian Ocean and separated from China by the Himalayan mountain range. Mount Everest, the highest mountain in the world at 29,028 feet (8,848 meters), is in the Himalayas on the border between Nepal and China.

India is the biggest country in the region, while the Maldives, in the Indian Ocean, is the smallest.

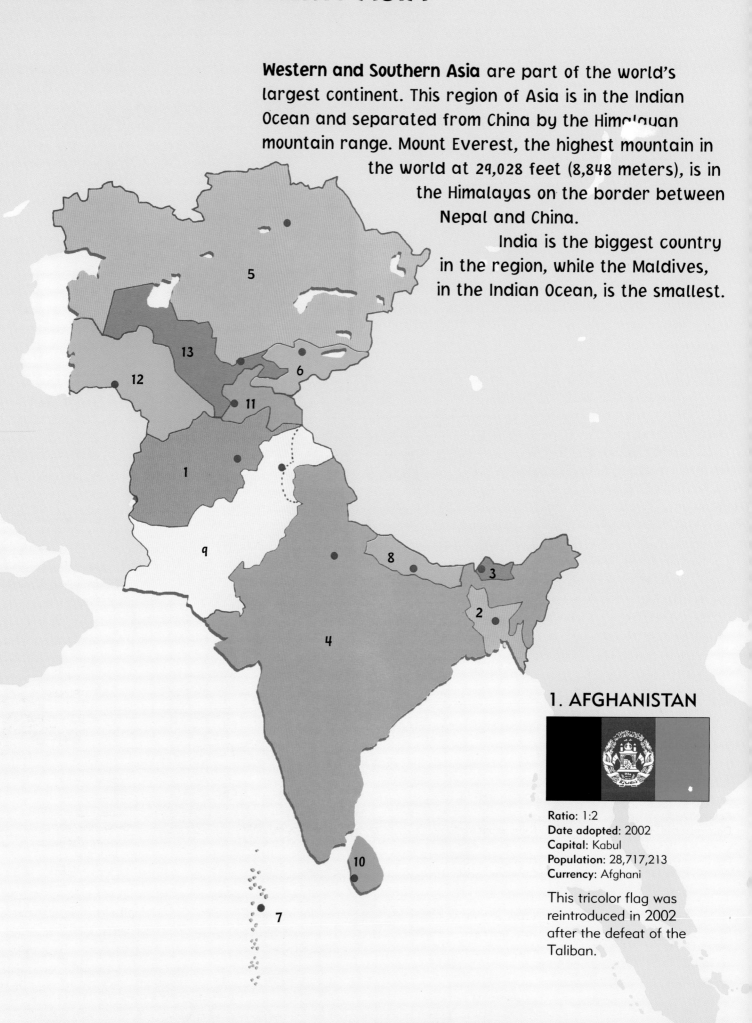

1. AFGHANISTAN

Ratio: 1:2
Date adopted: 2002
Capital: Kabul
Population: 28,717,213
Currency: Afghani

This tricolor flag was reintroduced in 2002 after the defeat of the Taliban.

2. BANGLADESH

Ratio: 3:5
Date adopted: 1972
Capital: Dhaka
Population: 138,___10
Currency: Bangladesh taka

The red disc represents the struggle for independence. The green symbolizes the land.

3. BHUTAN

Ratio: 2:3
Date adopted: 1969
Capital: Thimphu
Population: 2,139,549
Currency: Ngultrum

This shows the Bhutanese name for the country: "Land of the Thunder Dragon."

4. INDIA

Ratio: 2:3
Date adopted: 1947
Capital: New Delhi
Population: 1,049,700,118
Currency: Indian rupee

The blue wheel on the white band is the Dharma Chakra, "The Wheel of Law."

5. KAZAKHSTAN

Ratio: 1:2
Date adopted: 1992
Capital: Astana
Population: 16,763,795
Currency: Tenge

This flag was adopted after it became independent from the Soviet Union in 1991.

6. KYRGYZSTAN

Ratio: 3:5
Date adopted: 1992
Capital: Bishkek
Population: 4,892,808
Currency: Kyrgyzstan som

At the center of the sun is a yurt (tent), the traditional home of the Kyrgyz nomads.

7. MALDIVES

Ratio: 2:3
Date adopted: 1965
Capital: Male
Population: 329,684
Currency: Maldivian rufiyaa

The white crescent on a green rectangle stands for the Islamic faith of the Maldives.

8. NEPAL

Ratio: 4:3
Date adopted: 1962
Capital: Kathmandu
Population: 26,469,569
Currency: Nepalese rupee

The Nepalese flag is the only national flag that is not a rectangle or square.

9. PAKISTAN

Ratio: 2:3
Date adopted: 1947
Capital: Islamabad
Population: 150,694,740
Currency: Pakistani rupee

The white strip on the left represents Pakistan's religious minorities.

10. SRI LANKA

Ratio: 1:2
Date adopted: 1951
Capital: Colombo
Population: 19,742,439
Currency: Sri Lanka rupee

The lion and sword represent justice, while the four leaves represent Buddhism.

11. TAJIKISTAN

Ratio: 1:2
Date adopted: 1992
Capital: Dushanbe
Population: 6,863,752
Currency: Ruble

The gold crown and five stars stand for independence, which was gained in 1991.

12. TURKMENISTAN

Ratio: 1:2
Date adopted: 2001
Capital: Ashkhabad
Population: 4,775,544
Currency: Manat

The decoration shows carpet designs from the five regions of Turkmenistan.

13. UZBEKISTAN

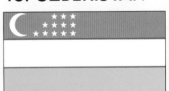

Ratio: 1:2
Date adopted: 1991
Capital: Tashkent
Population: 25,981,647
Currency: Som

The twelve stars next to the Islamic crescent represent the twelve months of the year.

EAST AND SOUTHEAST ASIA

East and Southeast Asia lie between the Pacific and Indian Oceans. China, at 3,705,387 square miles (9,596,961 square kilometers), is the largest country in the region and the third largest in the world. It is home to the Great Wall of China, a 2,000-year-old frontier that winds 2,550 miles (4,100 kilometers) across Northern China.

Singapore, a collection of islands between Malaysia and Indonesia, is the smallest country in the region at 264 square miles (683 square kilometers).

1. BRUNEI

Ratio: 1:2
Date adopted: 1959
Capital: Bandar Seri Begawan
Population: 358,098
Currency: Bruneian dollar

The script says "Always Render Service by God's Guidance."

2. CAMBODIA

Ratio: 2:3
Date adopted: 1948
Capital: Phnom Penh
Population: 13,124,764
Currency: Riel

This flag, showing the Anghor Wat temple, was reintroduced in 1993.

3. CHINA

Ratio: 2:3
Date adopted: 1949
Capital: Beijing
Population: 1,286,975,468
Currency: Yuan

The red background and large gold star represent communism.

4. EAST TIMOR

Ratio: 1:2
Date adopted: 2002
Capital: Dili
Population: 997,853
Currency: Indonesian rupiah

This flag was introduced when the country became independent in 2002.

5. HONG KONG

Ratio: 2:3
Date adopted: 1997
Capital: Victoria
Population: 7,394,170
Currency: Hong Kong dollar

This regional flag was adapted when Hong Kong reverted to China in 1997.

6. INDONESIA

Ratio: 2:3
Date adopted: 1945
Capital: Jakarta
Population: 234,893,453
Currency: Indonesian rupiah

Red stands for the physical world, and white for the spiritual.

7. JAPAN

Ratio: 7:10
Date adopted: 1870
Capital: Tokyo
Population: 127,214,499
Currency: Yen

This flag celebrates the fact that Japan is called "Land of the Rising Sun."

8. LAOS

Ratio: 2:3
Date adopted: 1975
Capital: Vientiane
Population: 5,921,545
Currency: Kip

The blue stripe represents the Mekong River that flows through Laos.

9. MALAYSIA

Ratio: 1:2
Date adopted: 1963
Capital: Kuala Lumpur
Population: 23,092,940
Currency: Ringgit

The fourteen stripes represent the fourteen states of the Federation.

10. MONGOLIA

Ratio: 1:2
Date adopted: 1992
Capital: Ulan Bator
Population: 2,712,315
Currency: Tugrik

The yellow design on the left is an ancient Mongolian symbol.

11. MYANMAR

Ratio: 6:11
Date adopted: 1974
Capital: Rangoon
Population: 42,510,537
Currency: Kyat

The rice in the emblem stands for farming, and the cogwheel for industry.

12. NORTH KOREA

Ratio: 1:2
Date adopted: 1948
Capital: Pyongyang
Population: 22,466,481
Currency: North Korean won

The flag was adopted when North Korea became an independent communist state

13. PHILIPPINES

Ratio: 1:2
Date adopted: 1898
Capital: Manila
Population: 84,619,974
Currency: Philippine peso

The three stars represent the regions of Luzon, the Visayas, and Mindanao.

14. SINGAPORE

Ratio: 2:3
Date adopted: 1959
Capital: Singapore City
Population: 4,608,595
Currency: Singapore dollar

The five stars stand for democracy, peace, equality, justice, and progress.

10

12

7

3

15

16

5

18

11

8

13

17

2

1

9

14

6

4

15. SOUTH KOREA

Ratio: 2:3
Date adopted: 1950
Capital: Seoul
Population: 48,289,037
Currency: South Korean won

The yin-yang sign symbolizes harmony, and the lines the four elements.

16. TAIWAN

Ratio: 1:2
Date adopted: 1928
Capital: Taipei
Population: 22,603,001
Currency: Taiwan dollar

Taiwan kept this former Chinese flag when it split from China in 1949.

17. THAILAND

Ratio: 2:3
Date adopted: 1917
Capital: Bangkok
Population: 64,265,276
Currency: Thai baht

During World War 1 the blue was added to show solidarity with the Allies.

18. VIETNAM

Ratio: 2:3
Date adopted: 1955
Capital: Hanoi
Population: 81,624,716
Currency: Dong

The red background and the star are both symbols of communism.

NORTH AND WEST AFRICA

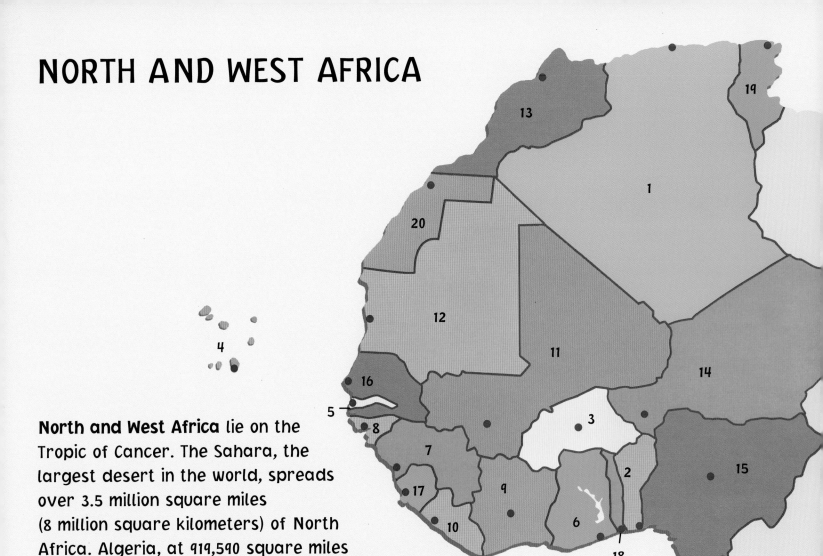

North and West Africa lie on the Tropic of Cancer. The Sahara, the largest desert in the world, spreads over 3.5 million square miles (8 million square kilometers) of North Africa. Algeria, at 919,590 square miles (2,381,741 square kilometers), is the largest country in this region. Gambia is the smallest country, at 4,361 square miles (11,295 square kilometers).

Much of the region was once ruled by Europe. Some flags reflect this, while others symbolize the struggle for independence. To show African unity, many have adopted the Pan-African colors (green, yellow, and red) of Ethiopia, Africa's oldest independent nation.

1. ALGERIA

Ratio: 2:3
Date adopted: 1962
Capital: Algiers
Population: 32,818,500
Currency: Algerian dinar

The crescent and star are symbols of Islam from the Ottoman Empire.

2. BENIN

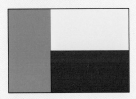

Ratio: 2:3
Date adopted: 1959
Capital: Porto-Novo
Population: 7,041,490
Currency: CFA franc

Red, yellow, and green stand for African unity.

3. BURKINA FASO

Ratio: 2:3
Date adopted: 1984
Capital: Ouagadougou
Population: 13,228,460
Currency: CFA franc

This flag was adopted in 1984 when Upper Volta was renamed Burkina Faso.

4. CAPE VERDE

Ratio: 3:5
Date adopted: 1992
Capital: Praia
Population: 412,137
Currency: Cape Verdean escudo

The blue represents the sea, and the stars Cape Verde's ten main islands.

5. GAMBIA

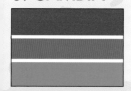

Ratio: 2:3
Date adopted: 1965
Capital: Banjul
Population: 1,501,050
Currency: Dalasi

Green stands for land, blue for the River Gambia, and red for the hot sun.

6. GHANA

Ratio: 2:3
Date adopted: 1957
Capital: Accra
Population: 20,467,747
Currency: Cedi

The star represents the guiding light in Africa's struggle for freedom.

7. GUINEA

Ratio: 2:3
Date adopted: 1958
Capital: Conakry
Population: 9,030,220
Currency: Guinean franc

As a former French colony, the flag is based on the French tricolore.

8. GUINEA-BISSAU

Ratio: 1:2
Date adopted: 1973
Capital: Bissau
Population: 1,360,827
Currency: CFA franc

The star stands for Africa and the red for the blood shed for independence.

9. IVORY COAST

Ratio: 2:3
Date adopted: 1959
Capital: Yamoussoukro
Population: 16,962,491
Currency: CFA franc

Orange stands for progress, white for unity, and green for hope.

10. LIBERIA

Ratio: 10:19
Date adopted: 1847
Capital: Monrovia
Population: 3,317,176
Currency: Liberian dollar

This flag is based on that of the USA, its former ruler.

11. MALI

Ratio: 2:3
Date adopted: 1961
Capital: Bamako
Population: 11,626,219
Currency: CFA franc

This flag combines Pan-African colors with the French tricolore design.

12. MAURITANIA

Ratio: 2:3
Date adopted: 1959
Capital: Nouakchott
Population: 2,912,584
Currency: Ouguiya

The symbols and green background reflect the country's Islamic faith.

13. MOROCCO

Ratio: 2:3
Date adopted: 1915
Capital: Rabat
Population: 31,689,265
Currency: Moroccan dirham

The "Seal of Soloman" was added to the red background in 1915.

14. NIGER

Ratio: 2:3
Date adopted: 1959
Capital: Niamey
Population: 11,058,590
Currency: CFA franc

The orange disc in the middle represents Niger's hot sun.

15. NIGERIA

Ratio: 1:2
Date adopted: 1960
Capital: Abuja
Population: 133,881,703
Currency: Naira

This flag was the winning entry in a national competition.

16. SENEGAL

Ratio: 2:3
Date adopted: 1960
Capital: Dakar
Population: 10,580,307
Currency: CFA franc

The five-pointed star represents unity and hope.

17. SIERRA LEONE

Ratio: 2:3
Date adopted: 1961
Capital: Freetown
Population: 5,732,681
Currency: Leone

Green represents its land, blue its sea, and white its wish for peace.

18. TOGO

Ratio: 3:5
Date adopted: 1960
Capital: Lomé
Population: 5,429,299
Currency: CFA franc

The stripes show the five regions of Togo. The star is for hope.

19. TUNISIA

Ratio: 2:3
Date adopted: 1835
Capital: Tunis
Population: 9,924,742
Currency: Tunisian dinar

This is similar to the flag of the Turks, who once ruled Tunisia.

20. WESTERN SAHARA

Ratio: 1:2
Date adopted: unofficial
Capital: Laâyoune
Population: 261,794
Currency: Moroccan dirham

Western Sahara is a disputed territory governed from Morocco.

NORTHEAST AFRICA

Northeast Africa lies on the Equator beside the Indian Ocean and the Red Sea. The world's longest river, the Nile, runs 4,160 miles (6,693 kilometers) through the region.

Sudan, the largest country in Africa at 967,494 square miles (2,505,813 square kilometers), covers much of the upper Nile Basin. Djibouti, in the Gulf of Guinea, is the smallest country in the region at 8,872.63 square miles (22,980 square kilometers).

1. BURUNDI

Ratio: 2:3
Date adopted: 1967
Capital: Bujumbura
Population: 6,096,156
Currency: Burundi franc

The stars represent the three main peoples of Burundi, the Tutsi, Hutu, and Twa.

2. CAMEROON

Ratio: 2:3
Date adopted: 1975
Capital: Yaoundé
Population: 15,746,179
Currency: CFA franc

The five-pointed yellow star, added to the red stripe in 1961, stands for national unity.

3. CENTRAL AFRICAN REPUBLIC

Ratio: 3:5
Date adopted: 1958
Capital: Bangui
Population: 3,683,538
Currency: CFA franc

The Pan-African colours are combined with blue from the French flag, as a reminder of its past.

4. CHAD

Ratio: 2:3
Date adopted: 1959
Capital: N'djamena
Population: 9,253,493
Currency: CFA franc

Blue stands for sky and water, yellow for sun and desert, red for bravery and freedom.

5. CONGO

Ratio: 2:3
Date adopted: 1958
Capital: Brazzaville
Population: 2,954,258
Currency: CFA franc

The unique diagonal design distinguishes the Congo's flag from other African flags.

6. DEMOCRACTIC REPUBLIC OF CON(

Ratio: 2:3
Date adopted: 1960
Capital: Kinshasa
Population: 56,625,039
Currency: Congolese franc

Formerly called Zäire, DRC readopted this flag after a military take-over in 1997.

7. DJIBOUTI

Ratio: 4:7
Date adopted: 1977
Capital: Djibouti
Population: 457,130
Currency: Djibouti franc

This is based on a banner used during the struggle for freedom from the French.

8. EGYPT

Ratio: 2:3
Date adopted: 1984
Capital: Cairo
Population: 74,718,797
Currency: Egyptian pound

The "Eagle of Saladin" represents a 12th-century sultan who fought Christian crusaders.

9. EQUATORIAL GUINEA

Ratio: 2:3
Date adopted: 1968
Capital: Malabo
Population: 510,473
Currency: CFA franc

The central emblem shows a silk cotton tree and the national motto.

10. ERITREA

Ratio: 1:2
Date adopted: 1995
Capital: Asmara
Population: 4,362,254
Currency: Nakfa

This flag was first used during Eritrea's fight for independence. The red symbolizes blood spilt.

11. ETHIOPIA

Ratio: 1:2
Date adopted: 1996
Capital: Addis Ababa
Population: 66,557,553
Currency: Ethiopian birr

These Pan-African colors represent the wish for African unity.

12. GABON

Ratio: 3:4
Date adopted: 1960
Capital: Libreville
Population: 1,321,560
Currency: CFA franc

The green stripe stands for Gabon's rainforests, the blue for its sea, and the yellow for the sun.

13. KENYA

Ratio: 2:3
Date adopted: 1963
Capital: Nairobi
Population: 31,639,091
Currency: Kenya shilling

The traditional Masai shield and two crossed spears are a symbol of freedom.

14. LIBYA

Ratio: 1:2
Date adopted: 1977
Capital: Tripoli
Population: 5,499,074
Currency: Libyan dinar

This is the only national flag using a single plain color. Green stands for Libya and Islam.

15. RWANDA

Ratio: 6:13
Date adopted: 2001
Capital: Kigali
Population: 7,810,056
Currency: Rwanda franc

A new flag was adopted in 2001 in an attempt to put Rwanda's troubled past behind it.

16. SÃO TOMÉ & PRÍNCIPE

Ratio: 1:2
Date adopted: 1975
Capital: São Tomé
Population: 175,883
Currency: Dobra

The two five-pointed black stars stand for the two islands of São Tomé and Príncipe.

17. SOMALIA

Ratio: 2:3
Date adopted: 1954
Capital: Mogadishu
Population: 8,025,190
Currency: Somali shilling

The five-pointed star stands for the five regions where Somali people live.

18. SUDAN

Ratio: 1:2
Date adopted: 1970
Capital: Khartoum
Population: 38,114,160
Currency: Sudanese dinar

This uses the Pan-Arab colors. The green triangle stands for Islam and prosperity.

19. UGANDA

Ratio: 2:3
Date adopted: 1962
Capital: Kampala
Population: 25,632,794
Currency: Uganda shilling

The great crested crane in the centre of the flag is Uganda's national bird.

CENTRAL AND SOUTHERN AFRICA

Central and Southern Africa lie on the Tropic of Capricorn between the Atlantic Ocean and the Indian Ocean. The highest mountain in the region is Mount Kilimanjaro on the border between Tanzania and Kenya. It is the highest point on the African continent at 19,304 feet (5,895 meters).

Angola, at 481,351 square miles (1,246,700 square kilometers), is the largest country in the region.

1. ANGOLA

Ratio: 2:3
Date adopted: 1975
Capital: Luanda
Population: 10,766,471
Currency: Kwanza

The cogwheel, machete and star stand for industry, agriculture, and progress.

2. BOTSWANA

Ratio: 2:3
Date adopted: 1966
Capital: Gaborone
Population: 1,573,267
Currency: Pula

The stripes of the zebra stand for peace between people of different races.

3. COMOROS

Ratio: 3:5
Date adopted: 2002
Capital: Moroni
Population: 632,948
Currency: Comoran franc

The crescent represents Islam, and the four stars represent the four islands of Comoros.

4. LESOTHO

Ratio: 2:3
Date adopted: 1987
Capital: Maseru
Population: 1,861,959
Currency: Loti

The brown silhouette is a group of traditional weapons: a shield, a spear, and a club.

5. MADAGASCAR

Ratio: 2:3
Date adopted: 1958
Capital: Antananarivo
Population: 16,979,744
Currency: Malagasy franc

Red and white are traditional colors. Green was added to represent hope.

6. MALAWI

Ratio: 2:3
Date adopted: 1964
Capital: Lilongwe
Population: 11,651,239
Currency: Malawian kwacha

The rising sun represents the dawning of a new age in African history.

7. MAURITIUS

Ratio: 2:3
Date adopted: 1968
Capital: Port Louis
Population: 1,210,447
Currency: Mauritian rupee

The four equal bands of color are taken from Mauritius' coat of arms.

8. MOZAMBIQUE

Ratio: 2:3
Date adopted: 1983
Capital: Maputo
Population: 17,479,266
Currency: Metical

On top of the yellow star sit the country's national symbols: a hoe, a book, and a rifle.

10 —

9. NAMIBIA

Ratio: 2:3
Date adopted: 1990
Capital: Windhoek
Population: 1,927,447
Currency: Namibian dollar, South African rand

The sun symbolizes life and energy, and the red band celebrates the heroism of its people.

10. SEYCHELLES

Ratio: 1:2
Date adopted: 1996
Capital: Victoria
Population: 80,469
Currency: Seychelles rupee

The rays stand for sky, sun, unity, justice, and nature.

11. SOUTH AFRICA

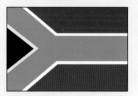

Ratio: 2:3
Date adopted: 1994
Capital: Pretoria
Population: 42,768,678
Currency: Rand

The yellow, black, and green are from the flag of the African National Congress.

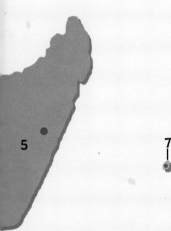

5

7

12. SWAZILAND

Ratio: 2:3
Date adopted: 1968
Capital: Mbabane
Population: 1,161,219
Currency: Lilangeni

This flag shows a shield, two spears, and a staff, all symbols of Swaziland's defense.

13. TANZANIA

Ratio: 2:3
Date adopted: 1964
Capital: Dodoma
Population: 35,922,454
Currency: Tanzanian shilling

This flag was adopted when Tanganyika and Zanzibar united to form Tanzania.

14. ZAMBIA

Ratio: 2:3
Date adopted: 1964
Capital: Lusaka
Population: 10,307,333
Currency: Zambian kwacha

The eagle, representing freedom, comes from the Zambian national coat of arms.

15. ZIMBABWE

Ratio: 1:2
Date adopted: 1980
Capital: Harare
Population: 12,576,742
Currency: Zimbabwean dollar

The colors come from the Zimbabwe African National Union, which has ruled since 1980.

OCEANIA

Oceania is a group of islands in the Pacific Ocean. It includes Australia, New Zealand and New Guinea, as well as over a thousand smaller islands.

Australia, at 2,967,892 square miles (7,686,848 square kilometers), is the smallest continent but largest island in the world.

New Zealand is made up of two islands separated by the Cook Strait.

New Guinea, the third largest island in the world, is two separate regions: independent Papua New Guinea, and Irian Jaya, which belongs to Indonesia.

Although many of the other Pacific islands are tiny, most have now formed independent groups and have their own national flags.

1. AUSTRALIA

Ratio: 1:2
Date adopted: 1909
Capital: Canberra
Population: 19,731,984
Currency: Australian dollar

The "Union Jack" is used because Australia was once a British colony.

2. FIJI

Ratio: 1:2
Date adopted: 1970
Capital: Suva
Population: 868,531
Currency: Fijian dollar

The shield depicts images of Fijian life. It also reflects links with Britain.

3. KIRIBATI

Ratio: 1:2
Date adopted: 1979
Capital: Bairiki
Population: 98,549
Currency: Australian dollar

This shows a frigate bird flying over the sun as it rises in the Pacific Ocean.

4. MARSHALL ISLANDS

Ratio: 10:19
Date adopted: 1979
Capital: Majuro
Population: 56,429
Currency: U.S. dollar

Blue represents the Pacific, the beams its two island chains, the star its districts.

5. MICRONESIA

Ratio: 10:19
Date adopted: 1978
Capital: Palikir
Population: 108,143
Currency: U.S. dollar

The stars represent the four states of Micronesia, and the blue, the Pacific.

6. NAURU

Ratio: 1:2
Date adopted: 1968
Capital: No official capital
Population: 12,570
Currency: Australian dollar

The yellow line represents the equator, and the star Nauru's location.

7. NEW ZEALAND

Ratio: 1:2
Date adopted: 1902
Capital: Wellington
Population: 3,951,307
Currency: New Zealand dollar

The Southern Cross is used by many southern hemisphere countries.

8. PALAU

Ratio: 5:8
Date adopted: 1981
Capital: Koror
Population: 19,717
Currency: U.S. dollar

The yellow disc represents the full moon, the best time for harvest.

9. PAPUA NEW GUINEA

Ratio: 3:4
Date adopted: 1971
Capital: Port Moresby
Population: 5,295,816
Currency: Kina

The bird of paradise, a local emblem, is a symbol of independence.

10. SAMOA

Ratio: 1:2
Date adopted: 1949
Capital: Apia
Population: 178,173
Currency: Tala

Red, white, and blue stand for courage, purity, and freedom.

11. SOLOMON ISLANDS

Ratio: 1:2
Date adopted: 1977
Capital: Honiara
Population: 509,190
Currency: Solomon Islands dollar

The five stars represent the five main groups of islands.

12. TONGA

Ratio: 1:2
Date adopted: 1875
Capital: Nuku'alofa
Population: 108,141
Currency: Pa'anga

This flag symbolizes the Christian faith practiced in Tonga.

13. TUVALU

Ratio: 1:2
Date adopted: 1978
Capital: Funafuti
Population: 11,305
Currency: Australian dollar

The nine stars represent the nine islands in Tuvalu's island chain.

14. VANUATU

Ratio: 3:5
Date adopted: 1980
Capital: Port-Vila
Population: 199,414
Currency: Vatu

The boar's tusk and fern leaves are traditional Vanuatan symbols.

3

13

10

2

12

US STATE FLAGS

The United States of America stretches across North America. It is made up of fifty states, including the detached states of Alaska and Hawaii. The United States was first formed when thirteen states declared their independence from Britain in 1776. In the following years, the other states joined the Union.

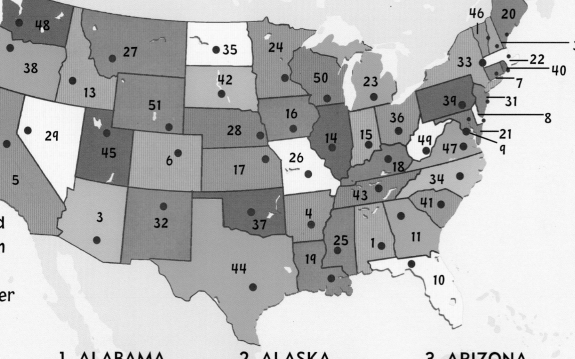

1. ALABAMA

Ratio: 1:1
Date adopted: 1895
Capital: Montgomery
Population: 4,352,000

Alabama's troops flew a similar flag during the Civil War.

2. ALASKA

Ratio: 2:3
Date adopted: 1959
Capital: Juneau
Population: 6141,000

The flag, designed in 1926, shows the Big Dipper and North Star.

3. ARIZONA

Ratio: 2:3
Date adopted: 1927
Capital: Phoenix
Population: 4,669,000

The copper star represents the copper produced in Arizona.

4. ARKANSAS

Ratio: 2:3
Date adopted: 1913
Capital: Little Rock
Population: 2,538,000

The diamond shape is used because Arkansas is the only state where diamonds are found.

5. CALIFORNIA

Ratio: 2:3
Date adopted: 1911
Capital: Sacramento
Population: 32,667,000

This shows a grizzly bear walking towards the star of freedom.

6. COLORADO

Ratio: 2:3
Date adopted: 1911
Capital: Denver
Population: 3,971,000

Gold represents the state's sunshine, white its mountains, blue its skies, and red its earth.

7. CONNECTICUT

Ratio: 4:5
Date adopted: 1897
Capital: Hartford
Population: 3,274,000

The motto on the bottom reads: "He Who Transplanted Sustains Us."

8. DELAWARE

Ratio: 3:4
Date adopted: 1913
Capital: Dover
Population: 744,000

December 7, 1787, the date beneath the state arms, is when Delaware joined the Union.

9. DISTRICT OF COLUMBIA

Ratio: 10:19
Date adopted: 1938
Capital: Washington, D.C.
Population: 606,900

This red-and-white flag is based on the coat of arms of George Washington.

10. FLORIDA

Ratio: 2:3
Date adopted: 1868
Capital: Tallahassee
Population: 14,916,000

The cross that the seal sits on is based on the Confederate flag used during the Civil War.

11. GEORGIA

Ratio: 2:3
Date adopted: 2003
Capital: Atlanta
Population: 7,642,000

The canton shows the seal of state, and 13 stars the first states of the union.

12. HAWAII

Ratio: 1:2
Date adopted: 1845
Capital: Honolulu
Population: 1,193,000

This combines the flags of the United States and the United Kingdom.

13. IDAHO

Ratio: 2:3
Date adopted: 1927
Capital: Boise
Population: 1,229,000

This is based on a flag used by Idaho soldiers during the Spanish-American war in 1899.

14. ILLINOIS

Ratio: 3:5
Date adopted: 1915
Capital: Springfield
Population: 12,045,000

The state name at the bottom was added in 1970 to ensure that the flag was recognized.

15. INDIANA

Ratio: 2:3
Date adopted: 1917
Capital: Indianapolis
Population: 5,899,000

The torch represents enlightenment and liberty. The star above it represents Indiana.

US STATE FLAGS

16. IOWA

Ratio: 2:3
Date adopted: 1962
Capital: Des Moines
Population: 2,862,000

The motto beneath the eagle says: "Our Liberties We Prize and Our Rights We Maintain."

17. KANSAS

Ratio: 3:5
Date adopted: 1925
Capital: Topeka
Population: 2,629,000

The sunflower at the top is the state flower. The motto is: "United We Stand, Divided We Fall."

18. KENTUCKY

Ratio: 2:3
Date adopted: 1918
Capital: Frankfort
Population: 3,937,000

Although this flag was adopted in 1918, it was not officially defined until 1963.

19. LOUISIANA

Ratio: 2:3
Date adopted: 1912
Capital: Baton Rouge
Population: 4,369,000

The Pelican represents self-sacrifice and Louisiana's role as a protector.

20. MAINE

Ratio: 2:3
Date adopted: 1909
Capital: Augusta
Population: 1,244,000

A farmer and a seaman stand either side of the central shield, featuring a pine tree and a moose.

21. MARYLAND

Ratio: 2:3
Date adopted: 1904
Capital: Annapolis
Population: 5,135,000

This flag was first used by a Maryland regiment in 1888 during a parade in Baltimore.

22. MASSACHUSETTS

Ratio: 2:3
Date adopted: 1908
Capital: Boston
Population: 5,817,000

At the center of this flag is a Native American holding a bow and arrow.

23. MICHIGAN

Ratio: 2:3
Date adopted: 1911
Capital: Lansing
Population: 9,088,000

The shield shows a frontiersman. The elk and moose are state symbols.

24. MINNESOTA

Ratio: 7:11
Date adopted: 1893
Capital: St Paul
Population: 4,725,000

The motto, "Star of the North", recalls the time when Minnesota was the northernmost state.

25. MISSISSIPPI

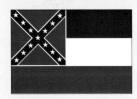

Ratio: 2:3
Date adopted: 1894
Capital: Jackson
Population: 2,752,000

The thirteen stars in the diagonal cross represent the thirteen original states.

26. MISSOURI

Ratio: 10:17
Date adopted: 1913
Capital: Jefferson City
Population: 5,439,000

The twenty-four stars around the circle show that Missouri was the twenty-fourth state.

27. MONTANA

Ratio: 2:3
Date adopted: 1905
Capital: Helena
Population: 880,000

The plough, miner's pick, and shovel represent Montana's agriculture and industry.

28. NEBRASKA

Ratio: 3:5
Date adopted: 1963
Capital: Lincoln
Population: 1,663,000

Nebraska was one of the last states in the United States to adopt a flag in 1963.

29. NEVADA

Ratio: 2:3
Date adopted: 1929
Capital: Carson City
Population: 1,747,000

The motto, "Battle Born," refers to the formation of the state during the Civil War.

30. NEW HAMPSHIRE

Ratio: 2:3
Date adopted: 1909
Capital: Concord
Population: 1,185,000

The seal shows the frigate, Raleigh, being built during the War of Independence.

31. NEW JERSEY

Ratio: 2:3
Date adopted: 1896
Capital: Trenton
Population: 8,115,000

The goddesses on either side of the seal stand for liberty and agriculture.

32. NEW MEXICO

Ratio: 2:3
Date adopted: 1925
Capital: Santa Fe
Population: 1,737,000

At the centre of this flag is the sun symbol of the Zia Pueblo Indians.

33. NEW YORK

Ratio: 1:2
Date adopted: 1901
Capital: Albany
Population: 18,175,000

The figures flanking the coat of arms are Liberty and Justice. Excelsior means 'higher'.

34. NORTH CAROLINA

Ratio: 2:3
Date adopted: 1885
Capital: Raleigh
Population: 7,546,000

May 20th, 1775 and April 12th, 1776 mark important dates in North Carolina's history.

35. NORTH DAKOTA

Ratio: 2:3
Date adopted: 1911
Capital: Bismarck
Population: 685,000

This is based on a regimental flag carried during the Spanish-American war of 1898.

36. OHIO

Ratio: 5:8
Date adopted: 1902
Capital: Columbus
Population: 11,209,000

The swallow-tail pennant, called the Ohio burgee, was designed by John Eisemann.

37. OKLAHOMA

Ratio: 2:3
Date adopted: 1907
Capital: Oklahoma City
Population: 3,347,000

The shield at the center honors sixty Native American groups and their ancestors.

38. OREGON

Ratio: 3:5
Date adopted: 1925
Capital: Salem
Population: 2,687,000

The date is the year Oregon joined the Union. A beaver is shown on the reverse.

39. PENNSYLVANIA

Ratio: 2:3
Date adopted: 1907
Capital: Harrisburg
Population: 12,001,000

The blue, which is the same as the blue used on the United States flag, signifies justice.

U.S. STATE FLAGS

40. RHODE ISLAND

Ratio: 1:1
Date adopted: 1897
Capital: Providence
Population: 988,000

The anchor emblem has been associated with this 'ocean state' since its foundation.

41. SOUTH CAROLINA

Ratio: 2:3
Date adopted: 1861
Capital: Columbia
Population: 3,836,000

The palmetto tree represents the defense of a log fort against the British in 1776.

42. SOUTH DAKOTA

Ratio: 3:5
Date adopted: 1963
Capital: Pierre
Population: 738,000

The motto, "Mount Rushmore State" is the state's nickname.

43. TENNESSEE

Ratio: 3:5
Date adopted: 1905
Capital: Nashville
Population: 5,431,000

The three stars represent the three parts of Tennessee: west, middle, and east.

44. TEXAS

Ratio: 2:3
Date adopted: 1839
Capital: Austin
Population: 19,760,000

This flag was used before Texas joined the Union and was called the Republic of Texas.

45. UTAH

Ratio: 2:3
Date adopted: 1913
Capital: Salt Lake City
Population: 2,100,000

The Great Seal of Utah contains a beehive in memory of Mormon settlers.

46. VERMONT

Ratio: 3:5
Date adopted: 1923
Capital: Montpelier
Population: 591,000

The arms at the center date from 1777-1791 when Vermont was independent.

47. VIRGINIA

Ratio: 7:11
Date adopted: 1861
Capital: Richmond
Population: 6,791,000

The seal symbolizes the Union's victory over the tyranny of George III of Great Britain.

48. WASHINGTON

Ratio: 2:3
Date adopted: 1923
Capital: Olympia
Population: 5,689,000

The picture on the seal is of George Washington, general and first president.

49. WEST VIRGINIA

Ratio: 10:19
Date adopted: 1929
Capital: Charleston
Population: 1,811,000

The coat of arms has a border of rhododendron, the state flower.

50. WISCONSIN

Ratio: 2:3
Date adopted: 1913
Capital: Madison
Population: 5,224,000

The date at the bottom shows when Wisconsin became part of the Union.

51. WYOMING

Ratio: 2:3
Date adopted: 1917
Capital: Cheyenne
Population: 481,000

The seal is shown on a bison, an animal which once roamed free over the Great Plains.

Canada is the northernmost part of North America. It is divided into ten provinces and three territories. It became independent in 1867 when four colonies united. In the following years, they were joined by the six other provinces and two territories.

1. ALBERTA

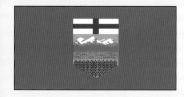

Ratio: 1:2
Date adopted: 1968
Capital: Edmonton
Population: 2,847,000

2. BRITISH COLUMBIA

Ratio: 3:5
Date adopted: 1960
Capital: Victoria
Population: 3,933,000

3. MANITOBA

Ratio: 1:2
Date adopted: 1966
Capital: Winnipeg
Population: 1,145,000

4. NEW BRUNSWICK

Ratio: 5:8
Date adopted: 1965
Capital: Fredericton
Population: 762,000

5. NEWFOUNDLAND & LABRADOR

Ratio: 1:2
Date adopted: 1980
Capital: St John's
Population: 563,000

6. NORTHWEST TERRITORIES

Ratio: 1:2
Date adopted: 1969
Capital: Yellowknife
Population: 40,000

7. NOVA SCOTIA

Ratio: 3:4
Date adopted: 1929
Capital: Halifax
Population: 947,000

8. NUNAVUT TERRITORY

Ratio: 9:16
Date adopted: 1999
Capital: Iqaluit
Population: 27,000

9. ONTARIO

Ratio: 1:2
Date adopted: 1965
Capital: Toronto
Population: 11,408,000

10. PRINCE EDWARD ISLAND

Ratio: 2:3
Date adopted: 1964
Capital: Charlottetown
Population: 137,000

11. QUEBEC

Ratio: 2:3
Date adopted: 1948
Capital: Québec
Population: 7,420,000

12. SASKATCHEWAN

Ratio: 1:2
Date adopted: 1964
Capital: Regina
Population: 1,024,000

13. YUKON TERRITORY

Ratio: 1:2
Date adopted: 1967
Capital: Whitehorse
Population: 32,000

U.K. NATIONAL FLAGS

The **United Kingdom** is in northwest Europe between the Atlantic Ocean and the North Sea. It is separated from the rest of Europe by the English Channel. It is made up of the kingdoms of England and Scotland, the principality of Wales, the province of Northern Ireland, and a number of smaller islands.

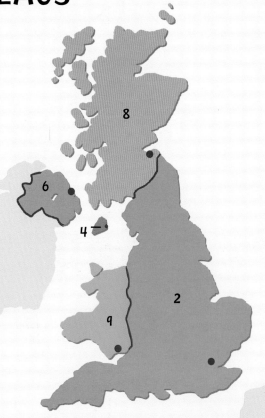

1. ALDERNEY

Ratio: 3:5
Date adopted: 1906
Capital: St Anne
Population: 2,086

Although a dependency of Guernsey, Alderney has its own flag.

2. ENGLAND

Ratio: 3.5
Date adopted: 1277
Capital: London
Population: 49,139,000

This red cross on a white field is known as the St. George's Cross.

3. GUERNSEY

Ratio: 2:3
Date adopted: 1962
Capital: St. Peter Port
Population: 60,000

The gold cross was added to distinguish it from the English flag.

4. ISLE OF MAN

Ratio: 1.2
Date adopted: 1971
Capital: Douglas
Population: 64,679

The three legs in the middle are known as the "Trinacria."

5. JERSEY

Ratio: 3.5
Date adopted: 1981
Capital: St. Helier
Population: 84,000

The coat of arms above the red cross was added in 1981.

6. NORTHERN IRELAND

Ratio: 1.2
Date adopted: 1973
Capital: Belfast
Population: 1,685,267

The Union Jack is currently the official flag of Northern Ireland.

7. SARK

Ratio: 3:5
Date adopted: 1938
Capital: L'Ecluse
Population: 620

Sark is a dependency of Guernsey, but it flies its own flag.

8. SCOTLAND

Ratio: 3.5
Date adopted: 1512
Capital: Edinburgh
Population: 5,062,000

The St. Andrew's Cross is one of the oldest national flags.

9. WALES

Ratio: 3.5
Date adopted: 1959
Capital: Cardiff
Population: 2,903,000

The Red Dragon breathing fire is an ancient Welsh symbol.

AUSTRALIAN STATE FLAGS

Australia, the world's smallest continent, is an island state between the Indian, Pacific, and Southern Oceans. It is divided into six states and two territories. The states all show the British Blue Ensign as part of their flag.

ABORIGINAL FLAG

1. AUSTRALIAN CAPITAL TERRITORY

Ratio: 1:2
Date adopted: 1993
Capital: Canberra
Population: 311,000

The stars on the left form the Southern Cross constellation.

2. NEW SOUTH WALES

Ratio: 2:3
Date adopted: 1876
Capital: Sydney
Population: 6,371,000

The badge combines the St. George's Cross with a lion and stars.

3. NORTHERN TERRITORY

Ratio: 2:3
Date adopted: 1978
Capital: Darwin
Population: 210,000

This combines the official Territory colors: black, white, and ochre.

4. QUEENSLAND

Ratio: 2:3
Date adopted: 1875
Capital: Brisbane
Population: 3,655,000

The badge features the Maltese Cross and the Royal Crown.

5. SOUTH AUSTRALIA

Ratio: 2:3
Date adopted: 1904
Capital: Adelaide
Population: 1,467,000

The state badge shows a piping shrike on a yellow disc.

6. TASMANIA

Ratio: 2:3
Date adopted: 1875
Capital: Hobart
Population: 435,000

The red lion on a white disc recalls historical ties with Great Britain.

7. VICTORIA

Ratio: 2:3
Date adopted: 1910
Capital: Melbourne
Population: 4,644,000

This combines the Royal Crown with the Southern Cross.

8. WESTERN AUSTRALIA

Ratio: 2:3
Date adopted: 1953
Capital: Perth
Population: 1,851,000

The black swan recalls the state's first British Colony at Swan River.

INTERNATIONAL FLAGS

Many international organizations are easily identified by the flag they fly. Here is a selection of some of the more common flags from around the world.

ARAB LEAGUE

This flag represents a group of 21 Arab States and the Palestinian Liberation Organization.

A.S.E.A.N.

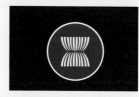

This is used to represent the Association of South-East Asian Nations.

C.A.R.I.C.O.M.

The Caribbean Community and Common Market was founded in 1973.

C.I.S.

The Commonwealth of Independent States is made up of former Soviet Union countries.

COMMONWEALTH

This is flown by countries belonging to the British Commonwealth.

EUROPEAN UNION

This flag is an expression of unity between countries in the European Union.

N.A.T.O.

The North Atlantic Treaty Organization is an international military alliance.

ST. JOHN AMBULANCE

The flag of St. John Ambulance is flown in Commonwealth countries and the USA.

O.A.S.

The flag of the Organization of American States shows the flags of all its members.

OLYMPIC MOVEMENT

The five rings which were first adopted in 1913 represent the five continents.

O.P.E.C.

This flag belongs to the Organization of Petroleum Exporting Countries.

RED CRESCENT

The Red Crescent is shown to protect medical units during conflict in Islamic countries.

RED CROSS

The Red Cross is shown to protect medical units during conflict in Christian countries.

PACIFIC COMMUNITY

The Pacific Community is an organization promoting economic interests in the Pacific.

UNITED NATIONS

The United Nations is an international peace-keeping organization.

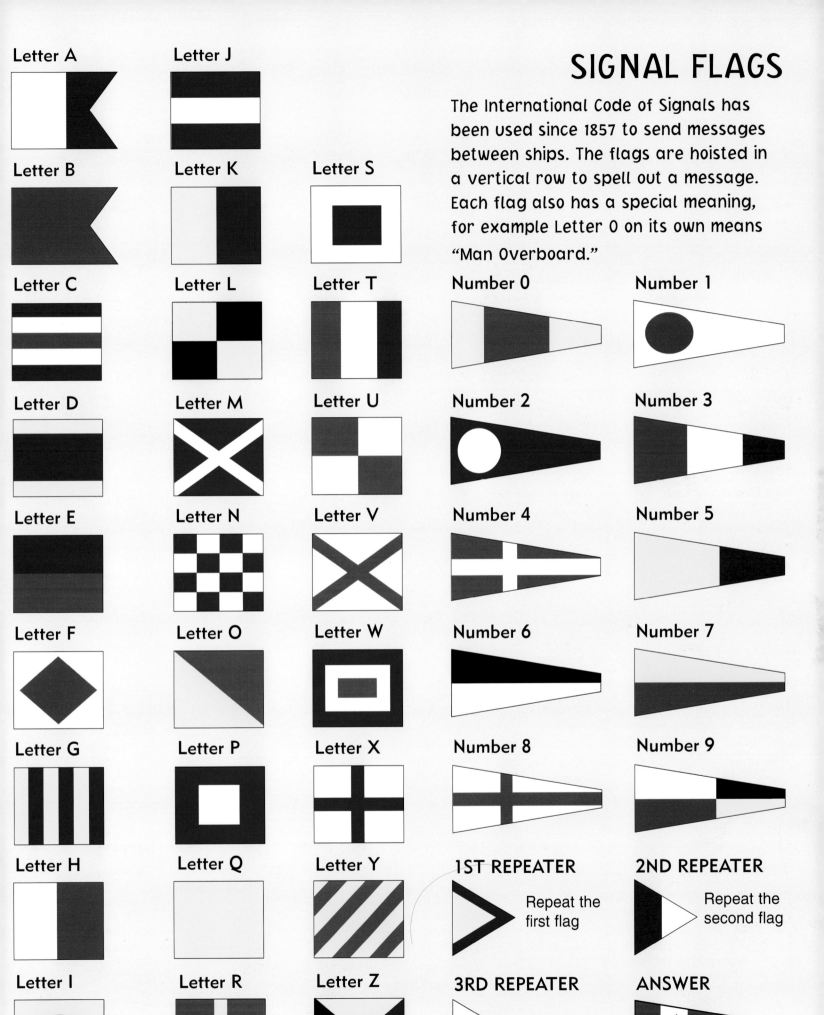

SIGNAL FLAGS

The International Code of Signals has been used since 1857 to send messages between ships. The flags are hoisted in a vertical row to spell out a message. Each flag also has a special meaning, for example Letter O on its own means "Man Overboard."

Letter A

Letter B

Letter C

Letter D

Letter E

Letter F

Letter G

Letter H

Letter I

Letter J

Letter K

Letter L

Letter M

Letter N

Letter O

Letter P

Letter Q

Letter R

Letter S

Letter T

Letter U

Letter V

Letter W

Letter X

Letter Y

Letter Z

Number 0

Number 1

Number 2

Number 3

Number 4

Number 5

Number 6

Number 7

Number 8

Number 9

1ST REPEATER Repeat the first flag

2ND REPEATER Repeat the second flag

3RD REPEATER Repeat the third flag

ANSWER End of message or decimal point

43

INDEX

GLOSSARY

CFA franc Communaute Financiere Africaine
coat of arms a badge or symbol of a city, noble family or nation
colony a settlement in a new country
communism a political idea that property should belong to all people to be shared equally
Crusader a Christian soldier who fought in the Holy Land in about 1000-1200 AD
dependency a territory belonging to a state that is usually in a separate location
ensign a flag or banner
federation a group of independent states that come together under federal government
Greek Orthodox the national church of Greece
Islam the religion of the followers of the Prophet
Mohammed Prophet of Islam born in 571 AD
Koran the sacred book of Islam
nomads a group of people or tribe who move around a region rather than live in one place
Ottoman Empire the Turkish Empire ruled by the Ottoman dynasty from 1350 to 1918
Pan African including all things African
Pan Arab including all things Arab
parish the towns or villages grouped around a particular church
Protestant followers of the Christian religion who do not accept the Pope as head of the Church
province a country or region usually part of a larger administrative center
religious minority followers of a religion that is not the main religion of the country they live in
Roman Catholic followers of the Christian religion who accept the Pope as head of the Church
solidarity unity and mutual support among people who have common interests
Soviet Union a large area of Eastern Europe including Russia that became communist in 1917
state the civil government or rule of a country
Taliban an Islamic military group who ruled Afghanistan from 1996 until 2002
territory an area of land under state rule
tricolore the French word for 'tricolor'
vexillum Roman standard flag

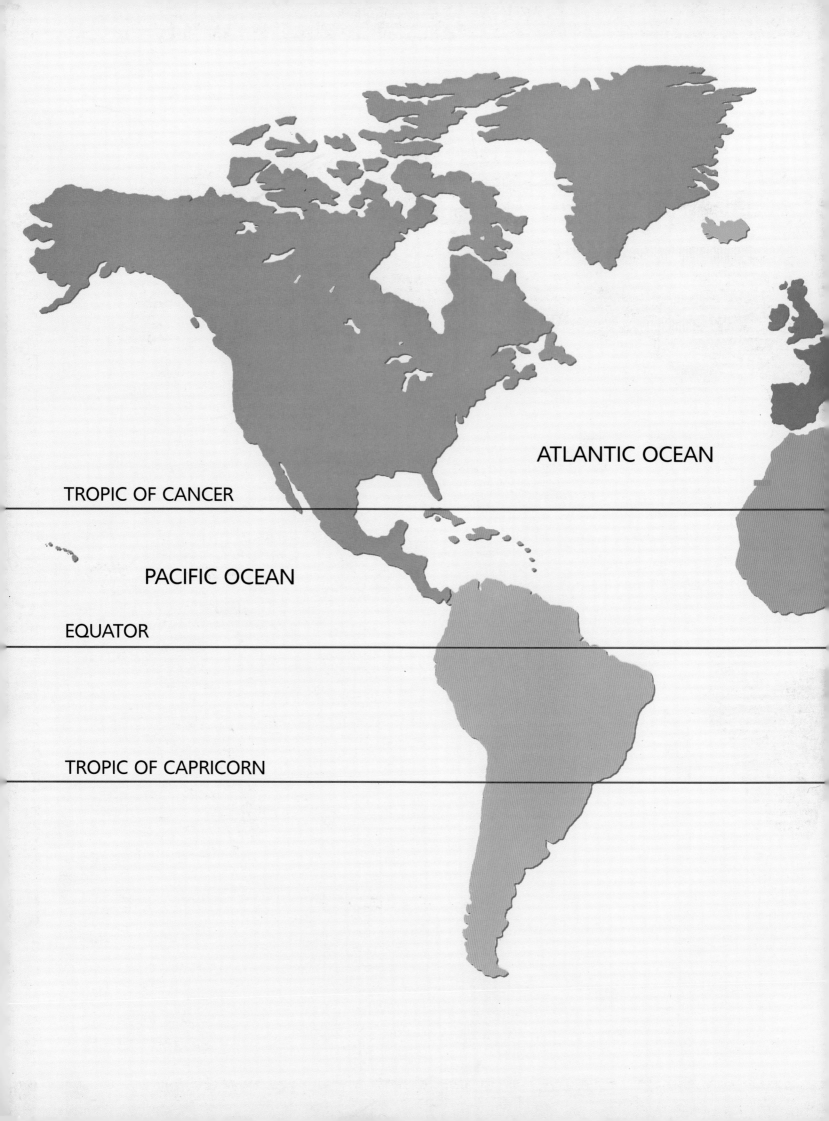

ATLANTIC OCEAN

TROPIC OF CANCER

PACIFIC OCEAN

EQUATOR

TROPIC OF CAPRICORN